THE AUNTIE NETWORK

Elenna Stauffer

BROADWAY PLAY PUBLISHING INC
New York
www.broadwayplaypublishing.com
info@broadwayplaypublishing.com

THE AUNTIE NETWORK
© Copyright 2023 Elenna Stauffer

Cover art by DALL-E

First edition: January 2023
I S B N: 978-0-88145-965-4

Book design: Marie Donovan
Page make-up: Adobe InDesign
Typeface: Palatino

THE AUNTIE NETWORK was developed at The
Studio Theatre Tierra del Sol and presented as a
streamed staged reading 14 August-18 September 2020.
The cast and creative contributors were:

TISH.. Roberta Emerson
BEX ....Leslie Munson
ANNE.. Matia Prescott
DES..Alyson Johnson

Director.. Nathaniel Niemi
Video Producer/Company Manager ....Ryan Loeckel
Set Designer..Kenneth Constant
Lighting Designer... David Krupla
Sound Designer ....Nick Erickson
Production Manager.............................. Danielle Paccione
Technical Director ....Clayton Becker
Stage Manager...Grace Zottig

SPECIAL THANKS

This play was originally titled SANCTUARY. Brooke Berman suggested the title it now bears, and has my thanks. I started submitting this play to reading and workshop opportunities just as the pandemic began, and by some magic, although ghostlights stood guard in theaters across the world, I got a letter from the marvelous Studio Theatre Tierra del Sol, asking me to be part of their virtual streamed play reading series. Though I only ever got to "meet" them on Zoom, the questions and insights from Nathaniel Niemi, Roberta Emerson, Leslie Munson, Alyson Johnson and Matia Prescott were helpful and necessary in shaping this piece, and I thank them also for their courage and can-do spirit as they navigated a safe way to make art in a very dark time. When thinking about the safety nets we build for ourselves and for each other I naturally thought about the people who have been part of mine, and I'd like to thank all the friends who have been there for me as a playwright and as a person. I'd like to thank the Lady Detectives, who read every page and offered insight, feedback and support. Thanks to Michelle Tattenbaum. Thanks to Natalie Kim, Victoria Myers, Kim Golding, and Adam Szymkowicz. Thanks to Mike Poblete (my brain). Thanks to the Yale Women Writers Screenwriting Group. Thanks to all the extraordinary women who are my own personal support network. And thanks, as always, to my family—all my in-laws and cousins and uncles and actual aunts. Thanks especially to my brother Ben, my Dad, my sister Amanda and my Mom, who all read and edited many drafts of this play and who support me with everything, always. Finally, writing a play about when and how one chooses to become a parent only makes me more grateful for the partner I have and the children we chose to have together. Jamie, Lily and Nicky, I love you always.

AUTHOR'S NOTE

The impulse to write this play came from a deep
interest in, and curiosity about, the limits of even
well-intentioned people's good intentions. Though
the restrictive abortion laws that pre-empted the
disastrous Supreme Court decision hadn't yet been
enacted, the warning signs abounded and the rhetoric
around abortion in this country suggested that many
Americans with the capacity to become pregnant might
soon lose the fundamental right to bodily autonomy.
I wanted to explore "the kindness of strangers," and
after re-watching *Rosemary's Baby* (of all things) a plot
suggested itself to me. But though I could see some
of the writing on the wall, I'm embarrassed to admit
I did not really believe we would land where we did,
and I have some ambivalence about the play not going
far enough. For anyone who shares my profound
grief at the injustice and inhumanity of Dobbs and the
subsequent states' restrictions, I'd like to remind you
of the existence of the National Network of Abortion
Funds, which lists the local on-the-ground groups that
have been doing the work safely and steadfastly (and
much less chaotically than the ad hoc efforts of Bex
and Tish and the fictional network depicted in this
play) and which will gratefully accept any financial
contributions.

CHARACTERS & SETTING

TISH, *female, 24, waitress and aspiring singer-songwriter, African American*

BEX, *female, 24, waitress and aspiring something, any ethnicity*

ANNE, *female, 16, blonde*

DES, *female, 35, more granola than the average building owner, any ethnicity*

All scenes take place in the common room of the crappy Manhattan-adjacent apartment where BEX *and* TISH *live. (Since they're newly graduated from college, it's more likely Brooklyn. Or Queens.)*

Scene 1

(A small common room in a very small apartment with a couch and a coffee table and some other slightly-better-than-dorm furniture. BEX, and TISH, recent college grads, lie on the rug on the floor looking at the ceiling. They are stoned.)

BEX: It's like...the *universe.*

TISH: I hear you.

BEX: Like how it's infinite? But...then, it might not be... We just can't see far enough to see where it ends.

TISH: Yeah. *(Beat)* But...hear me out.... If it does end? If it's, like, in a box? Then *what is outside of that box?*

BEX: That...is...deep.

TISH: Thanks.

BEX: That's, like, thinking outside the box. *(Beat)* Literally. *(Long, long beat.)* I love these talks.

TISH: Ditto.

BEX: Why can't this be my job?

TISH: Talking to me?

BEX: Doing something where I feel like the world is big and I am part of it. And, like, it's interesting and I want to be there. And I get benefits.

TISH: What about Anne? We are doing a good deed here. And, like, building bridges between... Oh. Haha. You mean for money. A job where you do good and make money... You could be...a shrink?

BEX: I would have to go to med school. Or some…
psychology grad school thing.

TISH: Okay. But, I mean, we'll have to go to some kind
of school. Eventually. I mean, you can't do anything
without grad school. We can't end up like Deedee.

BEX: Oh lord. No. I will not be a sixty-two year-old
waitress.

TISH: Is she really—?

BEX: Nor will you. We're going to do interesting things.
And meet interesting people. And get married. Or not.
And I'm writing a book, remember? And your album?
You don't need to go to grad school to be a rock star.

TISH: *(A little doubtful)* That's true…. Sure…I mean, it's
coming…I guess.

BEX: And in the meantime…free muffins!

TISH: So… I guess you can't actually say this job has no
benefits.

BEX: Muffins make everything worth it.

TISH: Even the terrible tourists. Who cares if they suck?
Muffins!

BEX: Muffins!

TISH: Seriously, though? Yesterday some Swedish lady
reached out to play with my hair.

BEX: Ew. Really? While you were serving her?

TISH: Yeah. But, you know, I'm from New Jersey. I can
put up with anything. Except, then she didn't tip me.

BEX: Stingy too? That's how I imagine the inhabitants
of Purgatory. Euroracist and stingy. Ugh. Swedish…
people.

TISH: Or maybe, like, Norwegian? She could have been
Danish, I guess. Or Belg…ish.

BEX: I hope you gave her *the look.*

TISH: I didn't want to waste my best material on her.

BEX: It's just my favorite, though. Really. I feel like if nothing else works out you could do, like, performance-art-slash-stand-up. You wouldn't have to say anything. You'd just, you know, give them the look, you'd terrify them, and then they'd cry laughing from relief and buy more drinks.

TISH: I don't know. No one else appreciates the look like you.

BEX: You should have tried it on the lady. She might have tipped a shit ton in fear. Or at least peed herself in karmic justice. *(Beat)* Didn't you say you were getting muffins?

TISH: I didn't… *(She rolls her eyes.)* You want some? They're in the fridge… You are so lazy. *(But she starts to get up anyway.)*

BEX: And high. I am so high.

TISH: *(Rolling her eyes affectionately. BEX always announces when she's stoned or inebriated.)* I know you are. *(She exits.)*

BEX: Hey, Tish?

TISH: *(From offstage)* I'm getting you a muffin. Chill out!

BEX: Is our ceiling messed up? Or is that, like, a vision?

TISH: *(Still offstage)* Messed up how?

BEX: *(She thinks.)* Bulgy.

(TISH enters, and hands BEX a bag of muffins.)

TISH: What do you mean, bulgy?

BEX: There. What is that? Or am I…?

TISH: Where? Shit. I think that's water. Like, water… damage…or something.

BEX: Like a bubble of water?

TISH: In the paint or plaster or whatever, yeah. I guess.

BEX: *(Goofy)* Should we pop it? Pop! Pop!

TISH: We should not. We want Des to keep renting to us, right? I'll just…mention it to her.

BEX: In writing. We should put it in writing. But nicely.

TISH: Look at you. Maybe you should be a *lawyer.*

BEX: But *nicely.* We have Anne here, remember… Hey, speaking of your music—

TISH: We weren't…

(Beat. It appears BEX may have forgotten her thought. TISH waits for an answer and when none comes she prompts:)

TISH: Okay. Speaking of my music…?

BEX: Oh! Yeah! When do I get to hear any of your new stuff?

TISH: I'm not sure it's… You want to?

BEX: Unless it's sad stuff. *(Truthfully)* I can't take anymore sad stuff.

TISH: I think it's more, like… fierce.

BEX: Cool. I like fierce.

TISH: One sec. *(She gets her guitar and starts strumming,)*

BEX: *(Listening, thinking. It isn't fierce)*

What's it about?

TISH: No idea. No words yet.

(TISH plays. It's okay. BEX is kind of into it. But it's not great by any stretch. But she is a very good friend. So she pretends. When the music stops, BEX pauses to "appreciate" it before speaking.)

BEX: *(Lying, but with good intentions)* That's killer! Really. You're gonna be famous.

TISH: You think?

BEX: Yeah. World is our oyster.

TISH: Mmm…what does that make us? Seawater?
Oyster guts?

BEX: *(Simply. Happily)* Pearls.

***

*(Hours later. BEX and TISH are curled up together on the
rug, still in the same clothing, asleep. ANNE enters. She sees
them and freezes. She doesn't know what to do, so finally
drops her bag on the floor to wake them. They startle awake.)*

ANNE: *(Entering, apologetic)* Oh! Sorry!

TISH: Mmph. What time is it?

ANNE: It's eight AM.

BEX: Jesus it's early. *(Realizing what she said)* Sorry!

ANNE: *(Concerned. Reacting to BEX's use of the Lord's
name)* Bex.

BEX: I'm sorry. Really. You just woke me up.

ANNE: I can see. I didn't realize…you two are…

TISH: We're what?

ANNE: Are you? I never thought to ask…

TISH: *(Realizing what she's asking, laughing)* Together?
No.

ANNE: Oh. *(Hurriedly)* I mean, I didn't—

BEX: *(Quickly, slightly preachy)* Not that there'd be
anything *wrong* with that.

(ANNE says nothing.)

BEX: *(Suddenly realizing how late/early it is)* Where were
you all night?

ANNE: Church.

BEX: No, really.

ANNE: Really.

TISH: Really?

ANNE: Yes.

TISH: All night church on a random Saturday.

ANNE: Yes.

BEX: They have that?

ANNE: It's true what they say. *(Wonderingly)* They have everything here.

TISH: I guess we're just used to...our *vices* being up all night. Not our virtues. *(She shrugs.)* I'm pretty sure my church isn't open all night.

ANNE: *(Thrilled)* You go to church?

TISH: Not till eleven.

(ANNE nods, relieved that TISH is, at least, a churchgoer.)

BEX: *(Suddenly worried, sitting up)* Are you okay?

ANNE: Yes. *(Slight beat)* Why?

BEX: I mean, that you needed to go to church all night.

ANNE: *(Genuine. With joy)* I love church! *(Slight beat. She can tell BEX and even TISH are a bit bewildered by her enthusiasm.)* This church was different. But still, it's more like home than anything else here.

BEX: *(With great sympathy)* Are you homesick?

ANNE: I don't think so. I just felt dis...connected. *(Eager to talk about her experience.)* It was... *(Struggling to describe it)* different than what I'm used to, but...it was good to be there. With God.

BEX: *(As motherly as she can be)* Well, it's only a few days, right? And then you'll be home before you know it. Do you want breakfast? You need to eat today, right? Keep up your strength? *(Turning to* Tish*)* We still have muffins, right?

Tish: I think we finished them.

Bex: Well, we have *English* muffins then. And I can scramble eggs?

Tish: There's a half a package of mushrooms on my shelf. Use those.

Bex: Okay! I'll put the coffee on, too.

Tish: *(Almost saying "God" but correcting herself midway through, for* Anne*'s benefit)* Yes. Thank Go-odness. For coffee.

Anne: I can make breakfast. I mean, I did just wake you up.

Bex: It's fine. I can get up. *(To* Tish, *teasing)* I'm not that lazy. *(To* Anne:*)* You hungry?

Anne: I ate at the fellowship breakfast.

*(*Bex *exits.)*

Tish: So you had a good night? A good morning?

Anne: *(To* Tish, *eager to continue the discussion)* Yes. But, wow. New York is…different.

Tish: Sure. But you get used to it. I remember the first time I took the subway alone.

Anne: Yes. There's a subway!

Tish: And how crowded it gets.

Anne: You could fit my whole town in three cars.

Tish: Really? Wow.

Anne: There must be dozens of churches here.

Tish: Hundreds probably.

Anne: *(Bubbling over with energy)* And yet the church was strangely empty. Our church is always full to

the rafters. *(Reverential)* When Pastor Evan speaks…
it's like the whole town breathes together. There isn't
an empty seat. Though we only have the one church.
Which church do you go to? *(With delight—she has an
intuition!)* Is it Baptist?

TISH: *(Her antennae are up.)* Methodist…

ANNE: *(Surprised)* Oh. Have you…always been a
Methodist?

TISH: *(Shrugging)* My parents are.

ANNE: There used to be a little Baptist church all the
way down Main Street. And all the women who went
there wore amazing hats.

TISH: *(Raising an eyebrow)* All the Black people who
went there?

ANNE: *(Trying to remember)* I don't… maybe? Anyhow
it's gone now. A lot of the other churches closed once
Pastor Evan started preaching. Our church welcomes
everyone. Pastor Evan says our church is the church for
all God's children.

TISH: Pastor Evan says so, huh?

ANNE: *(Blushing a little)* Everyone is welcome.
(Generously) You'd be welcome.

TISH: *(Unsettled)* Uh, okay. Thanks…

ANNE: As long as you were committed.

TISH: Well, you'd have to be, right? You were there all
night.

ANNE: *(Shaking her head)* This church was not like my
church. *(Trying to make sense of it, with wonder)* But it
was beautiful. It really takes the scripture to heart,
about washing the feet of the sinners and—

TISH: What, like you all washed each others' feet?

ANNE: We did. Yes. And—

TISH: Ewww! *(Calling to her:)* Bex!

(BEX enters, whisking eggs in a mixing bowl.)

BEX: What?

TISH: *(To ANNE:)* Tell her.

ANNE: About…?

TISH: What you just said. *(Beat)* About last night.

ANNE: *(Puzzled)* Oh. Just, that as part of the service… we washed the feet of our brethren as Jesus did.

BEX: *(Relatively unfazed)* Oh.

ANNE: It was beautiful. *(Sotto voce:)* I think one of the women… *(She considers.)* maybe a few of them, actually. *(Knowing she will shock them:)* I think they were prostitutes.

BEX: *(Not shocked. Shrugging)* It can be hard to tell. People in New York dress slutty.

ANNE: *(A beat as she considers. Then:)* I think the point was…that we're all sinners. And we're all capable of redemption. *(Beat. Then, with determination)* And I'm going to keep the baby.

TISH: You're…?

BEX: What?

ANNE: I'm going to stay here and have the baby. I'll give it to a poor childless couple on the Upper East Side—

BEX: *(Joking)* So not a poor couple.

TISH: I'm sorry. What?

BEX: Nobody's poor on the—

TISH: No. What she said. *(To ANNE:)* You're…?

ANNE: *(Reciting what she has decided overnight)* I'm going to grow my baby and then give her away. Or him. I was thinking. All night, whenever my mind wandered from the service. I will grow my baby "in perfect peace" until she can grow outside of me. And then I will "fix my gaze directly before me" and let her go.

TISH: *(Interrupting)* Hang on. Hang on. Wait a minute. What about...?

BEX: Yeah. What are you going to—?

TISH: No. I mean... *(Kindly)* I mean, you came here because you couldn't...? At home. You couldn't or you didn't want... So you came here...?

BEX: Are you sure this is what you want?

TISH: That. *(Gently, to* ANNE*:)* Look, you planned it all out and came here, right? So maybe you're just panicking? I mean, you didn't sleep all night and—

ANNE: *(Smiling)* I'm sure of myself. I'm not going to change my mind again.

TISH: *(Uncertain)* Okay.

ANNE: *(Firmly)* I'm going to stay here and have the baby.

TISH: You're going to stay...in New York...?

ANNE: I'd like to. *(Beat. Going for it)* I'd like to stay here. With you. If that's okay? Just until the baby comes? I don't know anyone else here. And I can't go back. Please. *(She looks at them both.)* Please? Just until the baby comes?

BEX: Until the...

TISH: I don't think... What are you going to tell your parents? You think they're going to let you stay here for all these months?

ANNE: I figured it all out during worship. I'm going to return to them after and say I'd been kidnapped but I got away, and I'm all right now, and—

TISH: Absolutely not.

BEX: Yeah, no. You're kidding right?

ANNE: I'll say I escaped my captors and then made it home. See?

TISH: And then when the FBI gets involved and retraces your steps what do you think will happen? They'll come here. And, like, we'll be arrested for kidnapping. Or worse. I don't know if you've been following the news or what the news even looks like where you come from. But I'm sorry. There is no way this ends well. Not for me.

BEX: Yeah. We are *not* doing this.

TISH: I don't even...Where do your parents think you are now?

(ANNE *shrugs.*)

TISH: Did you just run away?

ANNE: Sort of? ...Not really. "Aunt Jane" said as long as I'm heading home within forty-eight hours the police won't look for me.

TISH: But what about your parents?

BEX: Your parents won't look for you?

ANNE: I left them a note.

TISH: *(Incredulous)* You left them a note.

BEX: What did the note say?

ANNE: Since I was only going to have been here for the...procedure...we'd... "Aunt Jane" helped me make my story.

TISH: Which was?

ANNE: My first spiritual trial. My journey in the desert. *(In response to their confusion)* People do that. *(Beat)* Sometimes. *(Beat)* In my church. *(Beat)* It's a way of testing yourself and your faith. Some people never do it, but some do it every few years, to reaffirm their commitment. You isolate yourself from the community and from the world. Forty hours. One hour for each day he spent in the desert.

BEX: This is a thing?

ANNE: Sometimes people do it in the actual desert. Some people do it in abandoned buildings. Parked cars. Places where no one will find you.

TISH: And no one reports their missing kids?

ANNE: I left a note. But they'll expect me back after forty hours. Or so. So I need a different story.

TISH: You need to go home. If you're keeping the baby. *(Kindly)* You'll need your parents.

BEX: Yeah. You'll want your mom with you won't you?

ANNE: *(Vehemently)* They can NEVER know I'm pregnant. No one from home can. *(Beseeching)* Oh, please! I don't think I can do this alone.

(Long beat. When BEX and TISH don't answer, ANNE gets defensive.)

ANNE: Look, I know you were hoping to help some poor girl get rid of her baby, but… *(Sincerely, again)* You'd be helping me. You'd be helping us.

(BEX and TISH are stunned.)

BEX: Um…

ANNE: *(Gently sincere)* If you do support all women…? If you really believe it's our choice to make, my choice to make…?

TISH: Of course we do. But—

BEX: *(Firmly)* Of course we do.

TISH: Of course we do, *but…*

ANNE: Well…I choose this. But I can't have the baby at home, and I don't have anywhere else to go. *(When they don't immediately object:)* I'm so grateful. Thank you. You are… the very best of all the Samaritans. Thank you. *(She yawns.)* Maybe it's the baby or maybe it's the late night, but I'm very tired. Do you mind if I take my rest?

TISH: Wait wait wait. Wait. We haven't figured out what we're going to… I'm sorry, but the kidnapping plan is not happening.

BEX: Maybe we should call Mama Bear. For advice?

TISH: *(To ANNE)* Do you want to call your "Auntie?" Maybe that's the better…?

ANNE: I'm not allowed to call her anymore. Once I crossed state lines…

BEX: Look. At the very least, you need to send a letter home. So they don't think you've been kidnapped from your… journey?

TISH: Stamped from our post office? No way. *(She thinks. An idea comes.)* Hey. Here's a… Look. Until we figure this out… Could you say you are on a "mission"? From, like, your new church here?

BEX: But then, like, how did she get here?

ANNE: I WANDERED! Yes! Like Jesus in the desert. That is perfect. Oh, that's a great idea.

BEX: Is it?

ANNE: It's all worked out now! I feel so lucky to have met you both.

TISH: Wait wait. Hang on. Does that even make sense in your…?

ANNE: It's perfect!

TISH: Yeah?

BEX: But you can't forget to send a—

ANNE: I will. I will! From the post office near the
church. Oh thank you. I'm so grateful. Thank you.
Thank you. I feel lucky to have met you both. *(Before
anyone can raise any more objections she recites from
something she knows by heart.)*
"Womenkind is much maligned
From our birth 'til we're confined.
So together we are intertwined.
The prophet's flowers on one vine.
From rib to dust throughout all time."

(Beat. TISH and BEX are rendered speechless.)

ANNE: Does anyone need the shower before I lie down?

TISH: *(Startled out of her contemplation of ANNE's
recitation.)* Um. Yeah. I… Gimme a minute. I need to
shower before I go to church, but… I will…I'll shower
at the gym.

ANNE: *(Gently)* Hey. I realize I'm taking your bed for
longer than you expected. I could sleep in the living
room if that's better? For the rest of it?

TISH: Um. Yeah. I… No. Of course not. You're not
sleeping on the couch pregnant! It's…fine. Just let me
grab some things. *(She exits.)*

(BEX and ANNE stand smiling awkwardly at each other.)

ANNE: The Lord moves in mysterious ways.

BEX: Yeah… Do you…? Are…? Are you…? Do you…?
Should…?

(TISH returns.)

TISH: I'm good. It's all yours.

ANNE: Thank you.

BEX: Have a nice nap!

(ANNE *exits.* BEX *and* TISH *stand waiting a few minutes.*
Then from offstage they hear the whirr of a white noise
machine. They whisper intently.)

TISH: Holy shit! Holy shit! Holy shit!

BEX: I don't even… That was one creepy poem. Do
you think that people in her church, like…speak in
tongues?

TISH: Bex! Focus. She's keeping it! She was going to be
gone Tuesday. *(A realization)* Now…? What do we do?
This is nuts.

BEX: We…I mean…I guess… We're keeping…her? For
kind of a long time…

TISH: No. Hang on. Wait. *(Beat)* Okay. Okay. From our
training. What are we supposed to do? I mean, we
have to report it, right? Mama Bear needs to know. For
scheduling. Right?

BEX: I don't have any idea. I don't think there *is*
protocol for this. Is there?

TISH: I mean, probably not normally. But they'll know
what to do, right?

BEX: They will. Right?

TISH: But what happens when we tell them that she's
not getting an abortion? That our very first…

BEX: Our *first!*

TISH: Do you even think they'll send us someone else?
Later? After she…has the baby?

BEX: I have no idea. I mean, this probably never
happens.

TISH: They're going to think we're why she changed
her mind or, like, we let her be coerced by that foot-
washing church into…they'll never send us anyone

else. I can't believe we're keeping her here. We can't. We should tell her no.

BEX: But we just agreed.

TISH: We were in shock. This isn't how this is supposed to go!

BEX: Of course. *(Considering.)* But, I mean it would only be...is she three months or four? I don't understand the math.

TISH: Um. Mama Bear said she would be about twelve weeks. When she came. So that's twenty-eight weeks left. So that's...

BEX: Oh my God.

TISH: That's seven months.

(Beat. BEX and TISH consider.)

BEX: But, I mean, it's not forever... And we were going to host some other woman after she left. And then someone after that, right? So.

TISH: Yeah, but that's not the same. We can't. We don't even have a third bedroom. No. Bex, we can't.

BEX: *(Pleading a little)* I don't know. She needs us. Doesn't she? She's still a woman in need. It's just that now instead of a weekend...guest...she'd be more, like...

TISH: Long-term?

BEX: Right. Right?

TISH: We should call Mama Bear.

BEX: What's she going to say? I mean if she says, "great, thanks for hosting her, this sometimes happens and we're glad you're sticking with it" ...I mean...I guess the affirmation would be nice but...

TISH: Or maybe she says it never happens and it's not allowed and we have to tell her to go.

BEX: Go where? She said she can't go home. She's just a kid.

TISH: And her parents are going to think she ran away.

BEX: They're going to think she's on a Vision Quest. Desert Adventure. Whatever. We took her in because she needed our help. Otherwise The Network wouldn't have sent her to us. And, I mean…we're still saving her life. Maybe literally. *(She shivers.)* I mean, she can't have the baby there anyhow.

TISH: She may not want to but, I mean, having babies is still legal everywhere. It's *not* having them that's endangered.

BEX: *(Considering)* Well sure, but you heard all that… Adam's rib stuff…I don't get the sense she's going to be able to raise the baby at home.

TISH: I'm not saying she needs to raise it. I'm saying she could have it there and have it adopted.

BEX: And she said she can't… Come on. Isn't that literally the first step from the training? "We believe women." She's a fish out of water here, poor thing.

TISH: So let her go home!

BEX: Do you really think she'd choose to be here if she could have the baby somewhere else? She's not here for the museums, Tish! And we're…even if we're not literally *saving* her, we're good people doing a good thing.

TISH: You're making me feel like a bad person.

BEX: You're not! Are you kidding? You're a good person. We're helping her. Even if it's not what we imagined help would look like. In fact, don't you think that's even better? Because, like, if we only help people in the way we think they should want to be helped,

then isn't that, like condescending first world bullshit?
Aren't we part of the problem?

TISH: I mean…

BEX: So, we meet her where she is and help her how
she needs. It's, like, what… *(She struggles to remember
and gives up.)* …someone said in one of the meetings.
Or in, like, that ethics seminar I dropped out of junior
year? The discomfort is actually a sign that we're,
like…whatever, you know? *(Beat)* And, I mean, if you
think about it, it actually is a little creepy, right? To be
disappointed she doesn't want to kill it?

TISH: Bex. It isn't killing—

BEX: I know. I *know*. I just mean. Like, if she didn't have
it would we be happier for her? Is she right? I mean,
that's a little…right?

TISH: No. It's… We offered sanctuary to someone who
needs it. Who *(Reciting from training)* "found her way to
The Network because we are her last hope."

BEX: Sure. Well. And San Francisco. But we're closer.

TISH: Right. And we just weren't expecting… But.
Yeah. Okay. If you're okay with this, then I guess I
am. But we're going to make damn sure she sends that
letter!

BEX: Absolutely. I hear you. No kidnapping plots. And,
like, no loose ends, nothing that could put us, put you
in danger.

TISH: And, like, I don't want to have The Network
busted just because we're trying to… whatever you
said, "meet her where she is and help her how she
needs." I mean, it's—

BEX: I love you. You're such a good person. *(Cautiously,
conceding)* It is…unsettling though.

TISH: I mean. There are only so many safe places for women who need them. So if *she's* taking my bed then someone else—

BEX: Thank you, by the way. If you want me to give her my bed now that she's staying longer, we can…switch part way or something. You shouldn't have to have the couch the whole time…

TISH: We'll figure it out. I guess…

BEX: We will… We will. And just because this isn't what we…you know? Like our whole purpose—I mean, the only meaningful thing we're actually doing with our lives—is, like, making sure no one should have to bring an unwanted baby into the world.

TISH: *(Not sure where she's going)* Right…?

BEX: Well that's still true, then, right? I mean, this baby will be wanted, right? By the people who adopt it?

TISH: I guess. *(Darkly)* I mean I'm sure it's a desirable baby. Like a designer baby.

BEX: *(Agreeing; she hadn't thought of that.)* Probably. I mean, she's never cursed, so she's clearly never done drugs or smoked or drank, right?

TISH: Well…I'm not sure we can assume that. I mean, she did, you know, with some guy…

BEX: Oh my… *(She reflexively checks to be sure ANNE isn't in earshot.)* GOD. That's so true!

TISH: *(Joking)* You forgot how babies were made?

BEX: I just can't imagine *her* doing it.

TISH: Ew. You shouldn't. Anyhow, yes, I imagine her pretty blue-eyed newborn—

BEX: How do you know he or she's—

TISH: Really?

BEX: You're probably right.

TISH: Her beautiful Caucasoid baby will get snapped up and some couple that would have adopted a disabled biracial three-year-old won't now.

BEX: *(A beat. Sadly)* I think you're giving that couple too much credit. They were never adopting that other kid. They were always waiting for one like hers.

TISH: Probably…

BEX: It may not be what we planned, but we're doing a good thing. We are.

(TISH pauses suddenly deep in thought. BEX resumes whisking the eggs and turns to go back to the kitchen.)

TISH: Bex?

BEX: Yeah?

TISH: That was funny, wasn't it? How she said an Upper East Side couple.

BEX: Yeah, well, I mean, they have enough money, right? I mean, I'd rather someone in Tribeca raise my non-existent baby, because, you know, coolness. Or Williamsburg. But, come on. You know on the Upper East Side that kid is gonna have its own room.

TISH: Yeah. *(She's trying to figure something out.)* But how did *she* know that?

BEX: *(Shrugging)* Maybe it came up at all night church.

TISH: God. Can you imagine? Going to church all night long and washing the skanky feet of a bunch of prostitutes and—

BEX: *(Laughing at first and then feeling bad)* Tish! Hey. Prostitutes are women too. I mean, we'd host them if—

TISH: Of course we would. I'm just saying. *Open toed shoes all day. Feet.*

BEX: *(Starting to laugh again. She snorts and tries to calm herself.)* Stop! Shhh! I hope she can't hear us. She's going to think we're making fun of her. Come help me with the eggs.

(BEX *exits and* TISH *follows her out to the kitchen.*)

Scene 2

(*A few weeks later.* BEX *is sitting on the couch texting frantically on her phone.* TISH *opens the front door and enters.*)

TISH: *(Entering)* Hiya. *(She looks around.)* Is Anne...?

BEX: Out.

TISH: Where?

BEX: I don't know. Clinic? Church? Class?

TISH: Oh! Did she actually sign up for one? I know she—

BEX: I think so.

TISH: From that brochure she brought home? From, like, the subway kiosks?

BEX: I don't think? I don't know. Maybe it's a class at the church? I had to close last night, so I've only just woken up...

TISH: Ugh. Again?

BEX: Uh huh.

TISH: This place is a pigsty.

BEX: Then you don't want to go in my room.

TISH: She has my room. Why are her shoes all over the place?

BEX: I don't know.

TISH: Maybe we should, like, have a talk about ground rules?

BEX: Mm—hmm. Hang on a sec?

TISH: Everything okay?

BEX: Yeah. Kind of. Des finally texted me back. She wants to come and see the ceiling.

TISH: Okay.

BEX: Um, we can't right now. *Anne.*

TISH: Oh, right. So hold her off. Tell her we're jammed this week but maybe she could come Sunday morning? We know Anne will be at church then and we can just make up the couch…

BEX: Ok. *(She dashes off a message.)* Done. What were you saying?

TISH: Ground rules?

BEX: I mean it's messy, but…it's just temporary.

TISH: Not that temporary. And if she has all that… leisure time…to take a class, then…

BEX: I think we should be encouraging her to take classes. *(Finishing and tossing her phone down beside her. Sarcastically)* I mean, if it weren't for college I wouldn't have the joy of a shitty low paying restaurant job…

TISH: *(Consoling)* It's in service of the muse.

BEX: Whatever. But, I mean, she can't get a job, right? So classes are…I think it's admirable. I can't imagine I'd be taking classes if I were still in high school and, like, pregnant in a strange city.

TISH: I guess. *(Beat. She's thinking. Decides to go for it.)* About…being pregnant…? Hear me out, okay? I've been thinking. *(Beat. Deliberate)* Don't you think she looks tiny?

BEX: Well, she doesn't drink. *(Beat)* Maybe I should give up drinking.

TISH: I don't think she's abstaining for weight loss.

BEX: *(Missing the point)* No, I know. I mean, I'm glad she's not drinking while she's pregnant, since she's having the baby. And I'm not really going to give up drinking. I like it too much.

TISH: *(Shaking her head. Trying to be more direct)* Bex. You ever been with her to one of her appointments? Because—

BEX: No. *(Suddenly stricken.)* Why? Are we supposed to? In this case? It never... Damn it. I never even asked her if she wanted... *(Worried)* Do you think she's scared, going alone?

TISH: *(Considering)* I don't know. I never thought to ask. *(A solution to both problems:)* Maybe, just to be nice, we should...offer to go with her some time. Keep her company? I mean, if she was keeping it, if, let's say... she was married and...having this baby with her husband. And it was all above board. He'd be there to hold her hand and look at sonograms and stuff, right? So now...

BEX: I don't know... She might not want to be all "look at the sonogram!" though. Since she's giving it up.

TISH: We can offer. She can always say no.

(ANNE enters. She has a small shopping bag.)

TISH: Oh, hey. *(Noticing her bag.)* Have you been shopping?

ANNE: *(She pulls out a napkin with a donut inside.)* Fellowship leftovers. From church. I couldn't just let it go to waste, and... *(As if she's made a discovery)* I love donuts! I think they taste better here!

TISH: *(Fishing a little)* Or, maybe you're getting those *pregnancy* cravings?

ANNE: Maybe? I've just never tasted anything this good.

BEX: That is one fresh donut. It *smells* good.

ANNE: Especially after the subway. (*Shaking her head*) It's unbelievable that people can live like this.

TISH: (*Reaching for a segue; fishing*) Speaking of shopping, I was just thinking, you're gonna need maternity clothes soon, huh?

ANNE: I guess.

BEX: (*Misunderstanding the import of* TISH's *question*) Do you think your church might be able to help with…?

TISH: I mean, you're gonna get *big*.

BEX: Tish! (*To* ANNE, *indicating* TISH) She's really a very nice person. She was actually just saying we should offer to come with you to your next OB appointment! (*Generously*) And I think she's right. I mean, if I was here alone, without my family, I'd want company. So—

ANNE: (*Embarassed*) No.

TISH: No?

BEX: Oh.

ANNE: No thank you. You don't need to make a fuss. And I've put you out enough.

BEX: I understand…completely. I wondered if you might find it hard to feel celebratory since…

(ANNE *says nothing.*)

TISH: (*Gracious, shrugging*) We just wanted to offer.

ANNE: (*Suddenly fidgety*) I need to go lie down. My ankles swole up since I've been on my feet all day.

BEX: Poor you. Absolutely, go lie down.

TISH: Of course. Lie down. Sometime, though, we should talk about how the next few months are going to look, in terms of…

ANNE: In terms of... What do you mean? *(Suddenly concerned)* Oh my goodness...are you mad? ...Are you asking me to leave?

TISH: No! No no no. Of course not. It's just that if you're going to be here for so long, I mean...look, of course I know you don't have money for rent or anything...

ANNE: I only had what they gave me when they brought me to meet you. It's all gone now. I don't... should I get a job? I'm not really qualified to do anything. But I mean I can...I can look. On the internet? Is that where people find jobs?

BEX: *(Consoling)* It's okay. Really.

ANNE: Though...I worry it would be hard for me to find a job now... Especially since I'm not going to be here in about eight months. I'm not sure who'd hire—

TISH: Six months.

ANNE: I can't go home looking pregnant. I already mailed that letter— they think I'm on a mission.

BEX: Of course. That makes sense.

ANNE: *(Miserably)* Are you trying to get rid of me?

TISH: *(Chastened)* Anne. No. We want to protect you. And, *(She catches herself, narrowly avoiding saying "God")* Go-lly, please don't think we're trying to kick you out.

BEX: We'll find the money for this...

ANNE: I could do the chores? *(Suddenly as if in extreme physical discomfort, she winces.)* Tell me what I can do.

TISH: You know what? Don't worry about it. *(Slight beat)* I mean, if you start feeling up to, you know, pitching in with, like the cooking or the cleaning or, like, the laundry! Or whatever. Just pipe up. But... *(Sincerely)* I mean, you need to rest.

BEX: And we can do…whatever. Everything. I mean we were until you came, right?

ANNE: *(Gratefully)* Thank you. You are so kind. Truly. I'd heard terrible things about New Yorkers. But you know, you are really… *(She gets emotional.)* And you know what, if I can't get comfortable, I'll come back and maybe I can take the laundry to the basement.

BEX: No, no, no. It's too heavy. I'll do it. It's too heavy, really. You just rest. If you want to try to help out later when you're feeling up to it, great, but otherwise, you just take care of yourself and that baby!

ANNE: Thank you.

(ANNE spontaneously hugs both BEX and TISH and then exits to her room.)

(BEX and TISH look at each other and mouth things but neither can understand. Then the white noise machine starts up offstage and they speak in loud whispers.)

TISH: Well, now she's not doing anything. Ever.

BEX: She offered to! But we don't want her to overdo it and hurt herself. Or the baby. *(Thinking)* I shouldn't have said "baby". Do you think I made her sad?

TISH: No. I'm sure she knows what you…

BEX: You think so?

TISH: *(Sighing)* You're good people. I'm sure she didn't take it the wrong way. *(Preparing to get to work)* Well, if *we're* doing everything from here on out…

BEX: She said she'll pitch in when she's up to it.

TISH: You think she's going to get more comfortable as she gets bigger?

BEX: What could we do? Make her carry the laundry and risk hurting herself or the baby?

TISH: *(Grudgingly)* Of course not. *(Still processing)* I just…I mean, she made it all the way out to church and back.

BEX: *(Appropriating ANNE's way of speaking.)* But then her ankles swole up.

TISH: You're right. *(Sighing.)* But, just to be clear, we just negotiated that she's staying here an extra month or two after the baby comes, and then…not contributing at all, not even doing, like, basic…

BEX: Hey. It's not what we signed up for, but we're still helping a woman in a perilous position, you know? Do you remember how scared she seemed about going home and anyone knowing she'd been pregnant?

(BEX's phone dings. She reads her text:)

BEX: Des can't do Sundays.

(It dings again.)

BEX: And she's jammed the rest of this week. Doctor's visits, blah blah. *(Looking up:)* What should I say?

TISH: Find out when Anne's class is or just pick a time when one of us can be here and we'll ask Anne to go out until she's gone.

BEX: Okay. *(Musing)* I keep wondering where she's from, poor thing.

TISH: Here, no? The building's been in her family—

BEX: No. *Anne.*

TISH: *(Seriously)* We're not supposed to know.

BEX: I know. But I'm so curious! Do you think she has an accent? *(Shaking her head.)* I suck at accents.

TISH: *(Speaking aloud to herself more than to BEX)* On the other hand, maybe it doesn't matter now? I mean, if she *were* actually getting the abortion, of course we wouldn't want to know anything. It's how we protect her.

BEX: *(Why are you telling me this?)* I know.

TISH: But. Now she's not…and we still don't know her real name, where she's from, or really anything else about her.

BEX: Right. *(Confused by whatever TISH is insinuating).*

TISH: I don't know. It feels funny.

BEX: Well…all the rules and things weren't really made for this situation. Right? I mean, we could call The Number but what are they—

TISH: It's not an emergency. It's just…

BEX: Yeah.

TISH: Yeah.

BEX: Hey. Even if it's not what we expected, even if she's not what we expected, she got here through The Network, remember? I mean, they wouldn't have sent her to us if she had other options. We're doing a good thing.

TISH: *(Sighing)* You are a better person than I am.

BEX: No. I am not.

TISH: Nicer, then.

BEX: Well, you're a better cook, so it evens out.

TISH: *(Laughing a little)* I thought for a second you were going to say I was better at laundry so you could get out of it.

BEX: I would never! I would never have thought of such a genius thing. *(Sighing)* Too late, huh? But…it is actually kind of heavy, when it's three people's…I'd take a hand if…?

TISH: Happy to help. *(She gathers the rest of the stuff.)*

BEX: *(Bolstering her)* See! You you're always ready to pitch in.

TISH: Right! We're not suckers. We're…helpers.

BEX: *(Miming holding out a tray. Repeating the line their manager always says:)* "Here to serve."

(Rolling her eyes, TISH *opens the door and* BEX *and* TISH *exit.)*

Scene 3

(Three weeks later.)

BEX: Hey, Tish? Anne? Is anyone here?

*(*TISH *comes out of the kitchen.)*

TISH: What's the matter?

BEX: Nothing.

TISH: You sure?

BEX: I thought maybe I'd squeeze in a nap. If no one was here. I'm just fried. I feel like every single thing on my calendar is a huge impediment and I can't seem to get anything done and I'm just so tired.

TISH: Okay. Can I help?

BEX: No. I got my loan statement and I somehow owe more this month than I did last month. And my mom is on me to schedule a well visit while I have healthcare and I'm like, NO, I have healthcare because I'm too busy working to make it to the doctor! And, like, all the messages I have to return. And I have to change shift times again because I don't even know why. And Des hasn't called me back and I just want to be able to cross things off my to-do list!

TISH: She didn't get back to you? Want me to try her?

BEX: No. The ball's in her court now. I just wish she'd pick a time and show up and leave so I can stop worrying about clearing it with Anne's schedule. She'd said she could come at eight A M Tuesday, but Anne said she didn't have anywhere to be, and that seemed mean, to make her get up and out of here so early, not to mention if it was a morning when we could sleep in, that would just suck, so I called Des back and told her Tuesday wouldn't work but then she said if it wasn't an emergency that she couldn't come the rest of this week and we'd have to push it off again. She's *(She makes finger quotes.)* "very busy."

TISH: Are you mad?

BEX: I'm just. We're busy too, you know. And. Okay. She's not here, is she? Anne?

TISH: I think she's at some film screening her new student ID got her into?

BEX: She has a student ID now?

TISH: From her "New York in Film" class?

BEX: New York in Film?

TISH: Whatever it's called. Something like that. She's auditing some class someone from church connected her to? Anyhow.

BEX: Okay.

TISH: *(She shrugs.)* Maybe she's starting to like it here.

BEX: That's cool.

TISH: She's living her best life…

BEX: She is, isn't she?

TISH: *(Devil's advocate, sussing her out)* Well, I mean, we agree that she needs all the support she can get, right?

BEX: Of course. I want her to feel supported. *(Beat. Brave. Confessing)* Though, sometimes, I find myself thinking ungenerous thoughts. Like, "she can surely wash a mug when she finishes it, can't she?"

Tish: *(Agreeing. Gossipy)* I was trying to vacuum today—

Bex: Thank you!

Tish: You're welcome! Thank you for doing the dusting and the windows! I feel like it somehow gets dustier faster now. And messier. I don't even know how that's possible.

Bex: It's not as bad as your room. Her room.

Tish: Mm-hm. I wasn't sure you'd noticed. Something's just…off. I don't understand what she does all day that she's too busy to—

Bex: *(Conceding)* Well, she's pregnant. She naps a lot.

Tish: Is she though?

Bex: Napping?

Tish: No. *(Beat)* It's weird isn't it? How she's still so skinny?

Bex: *(Gossipy)* I actually think she's put on some weight.

Tish: Only because she's always trying a new ice cream place or eating the muffins we bring home.

Bex: Be nice.

Tish: I wonder if she's actually pregnant.

Bex: Really? *(She starts to laugh.)*

Tish: What?

Bex: She found us through The Network!

Tish: So? Maybe she wants an escape from her boring town and we seemed like easy marks.

Bex: What do you mean? She's never stolen from us.

TISH: Because we give her everything. She's literally wearing the shirt off your back.

BEX: It's loose. I thought she might like having it for layering. And I offered it.

TISH: Right. What if she's just, like, freeloading. Not pregnant.

BEX: But she's pregnant.

TISH: Have you seen a sonogram?

BEX: She's private! You've seen—she's very modest.

TISH: Or she's not pregnant.

BEX: Her boobs hurt.

TISH: She *says* they do.

BEX: So, what? You think she's just faking?

TISH: Or she's got a mental problem and, like, she *believes* she's pregnant but she isn't.

BEX: You know who sounds crazy now, right?

TISH: I would just like to see some proof.

BEX: Yeah, but I'm not sure how you get that without being creepy or invasive.

(ANNE *enters from the bedroom.*)

ANNE: *(Curious)* How you get what?

BEX: Oh! Hey! Where did you just come from?

ANNE: My room. I was resting.

TISH: I thought you were at a screening.

ANNE: Too achy.

TISH: *(Attempting to be casual)* Did you hear what we were saying?

ANNE: *(Lightly, teasing)* Why? Were you talking about me?

BEX: Yes.

ANNE: *(Taken aback)* Oh.

TISH: Bex!

BEX: *(To* TISH:*)* Well, we were. *(Turning to* ANNE. *Kindly)* We're sorry. We were just wondering if maybe something is unusual about this pregnancy. Like… you're very, very tiny.

ANNE: Thank you.

BEX: But maybe in a "is she *really* pregnant?" kind of way…

ANNE: *(Amused)* You know I am.

TISH: Do we?

ANNE: *(Joking)* You think I'm lying?

BEX: *(Trying to be helpful)* Or maybe crazy. That was one possibility.

ANNE: *(Brought up short)* I am not crazy. I am not lying. Why would I do that?

TISH: Free room and board? A place to crash in the most expensive city in the world…

ANNE: A chance to have the baby somewhere safe, where my whole life won't be ruined as a result. And yes, where a baby can grow up somewhere where it's okay to be anything, do anything. I want that for my baby.

TISH: I'm wondering if you ever even planned to abort the baby in the first place. If there even is a baby.

ANNE: I told you. You know I changed my… *(Realizing what* TISH *just said)* What?

TISH: Who sent you here?

ANNE: You know I can't give out personal details. "The Network depends on the security of its discrete links."

TISH: Yeah, but why do you care *now*?

ANNE: The Network offered me sanctuary. I'm not going to—

BEX: I'm glad that even though you changed your / mind—

TISH: Are you working for someone?

ANNE: …Like a job? No.

TISH: No. From…outside. From… *(A beat)* Lift up your shirt.

BEX: Tish!

TISH: Bex, I'm talking to Anne. I think that if we're going to continue this arrangement, that it's important we lay all our cards on the table.

ANNE: That sounds very threatening.

TISH: If you've got nothing to hide…?

ANNE: *(Anxious)* Are you serious?

BEX: *(To* ANNE:*)* It might be easier if you just show her.

ANNE: You're going to make me take my clothes off?

BEX: *(Helpfully)* Not all your clothes. Just enough that we can see your belly.

ANNE: I'm a private person. *(Slight beat. Clearly and deliberately)* It's my body.

BEX: *(Cringing)* When you say it like that… *(She glances at* TISH.*)*

TISH: It is. But if we're going to go out on a limb to protect your theoretical body as you incubate your theoretical baby, we have the right to / know—

ANNE: No. You don't. You can call your contact and trace it back to the first conversation I had, when I showed a woman my calendar and asked her what I needed to do.

TISH: How did you find this woman?

ANNE: I sat on a bench outside the dry cleaner's with my feet crossed at the ankles, carrying a yellow dress on a wire hanger.

BEX: That's...sort of gruesome and weirdly specific.

TISH: How did you know to do that?

ANNE: Facebook.

TISH: Seriously?

ANNE: Yes.

BEX: Seriously?

ANNE: There's a woman...she's...she was a stranger, but one day after church, she came up to me and a bunch of the girls on the playground. *(Slight beat)* And she told us that if ever we needed help, needed a "lifeline", that there were people to help us.

BEX: Okayyy?

ANNE: Somehow I remembered that.

BEX: That you had to go to the dry cleaner's with a yellow dress?

ANNE: No. That woman, she said that if we were ever in...a certain kind of trouble...she said Aunt Jane's Sale N' Swap would be our salvation. And, when I realized I was...in trouble...I found a reason to go to the library. They have computers there. And I searched and I found the page she'd told us about. And when I sent a message, "Aunt Jane" replied. Just as she'd said she would.

TISH: That all seems...implausible.

ANNE: It led me here.

BEX: It's very cloak and dagger, isn't it?

ANNE: Cloak and dagger?

TISH: Secretive and strange.

ANNE: Don't you see? It has to be.

TISH: *(Shaking her head)* These are some end times we're living in.

ANNE: That's what Pastor Evan says, too. May I go lie down?

BEX: Okay.

TISH: Hang on. You could have gone through all that without being pregnant.

ANNE: Yes. Yes I suppose I could have. But why would I? You have no idea what the world is like. You asked me when I came here what pronoun I use, for heaven's sake, but that kind of permissive-do-whatever-you-want-live-and-let-live, that is not how the rest of us are living.

TISH: So that's why you came here.

ANNE: I wouldn't have come here if I didn't need to. I don't need to be in a strange place where prostitutes go to church like normal people and no one cares if I'm married or not as my belly swells. I don't need to be an imposition, to be resented and gossiped about, asked to prove I am not a liar by the only two people who know me in this...Gomorrah. The only two people who, in theory, anyway, care about me. And *yet*. Somehow, because I've decided I can't go through with what I'd planned to do, because I've changed my mind and am going to carry this baby to full term and give her or him a shot at a better life, you are making me an enemy. And that is not a good way to be a friend. Or whatever it is you thought you were.

(Long beat)

TISH: Just lift your shirt, okay?

(ANNE, *furious, humiliated, lifts her shirt. She pushes down her pants, which were unbuttoned and hidden by a belly band. She pushes the band down around her hips. Her belly pokes out a little more. She starts to cry.*)

TISH: *(Satisfied)* Okay.

BEX: *(Relieved and trying to be soothing)* See? Now we're all on the same page.

TISH: *(Gently)* You can put your shirt down now.

(ANNE *stands motionless, crying.*)

BEX: We're sorry. You understand, we just...come on.

(BEX *starts toward* ANNE, *who flinches and recoils.*)

BEX: I was just going to help.

ANNE: Can I go?

(After a slight beat, ANNE *pulls up her pants and drops her shirt and goes to her room.* BEX *and* TISH *watch her go and even after her door slams, they look in that direction, considering. Eventually, they turn, a little guiltily, back towards each other.)*

TISH: We had to know. Otherwise she'd be taking space from someone who really needs it.

BEX: You're right. *(Beat)* I still feel a little bad, though.

TISH: Me too.

Scene 4

(A few days later. The doorbell rings. Long silence. It rings again. Another long silence. It does not appear anyone is coming to open the door. After another long silence, the doorbell rings again.)

*(*ANNE *reluctantly creeps into the living room. She looks around. No one is there. She is anxious. She creeps toward*

*the door to look out the peephole and bumps into an umbrella
stand, knocking one to the floor. She freezes.)*

(There's a knock.)

DES: *(OS)* Bex? Are you there? Tish? Are you in there?
I thought you said this time would work. Did I screw
up? *(She knocks again.)* Hello?

*(After a moment, ANNE resumes sneaking to the door to
peek through the peephole. Long beat)*

DES: *(OS) (Checking her phone)* Yeah, I have on my
calendar today at four. Did I get that wrong? Hello? I
heard you in there. Come on. I won't be long. Hello?
(She waits.) Look. I have…a lot going on, okay? And
I'm hopped up on hormones and I need to be home
by five-thirty, so…. If you're in there, can you…get
back to me so we can get this done? Just give me a few
options? *(Under her breath)* Milk of human kindness…

*(DES turns to go. ANNE watches intently. As DES starts
back down the stairs, ANNE unlocks the door.)*

Scene 5

*(A little over a month later. TISH is tidying up the living
room. Her things are in piles near the couch, which still has
her sheets on it. ANNE's belongings have taken up even more
of the room. BEX enters from the direction of ANNE's room,
carrying a tray with a partially-eaten sandwich, an empty
soup bowl and a flower.)*

BEX: *(Entering)* This is getting ridiculous.

TISH: I like the flower. Nice touch.

BEX: Thanks.

TISH: Nothing?

BEX: Nope. Outside the door. Like always. I knocked.
She didn't say anything.

TISH: Cold. Not even about the flower?

BEX: *(Trying to figure out where on the cluttered dining table she can set the tray)* Nope.

TISH: Damn. Did you tell her about the packages?

BEX: How could I? I guess she took them in though, when she took the tray. They aren't there now.

TISH: You left my note?

BEX: *(Finally setting down the tray)* I did.

TISH: She didn't leave one for me, huh?

BEX: Nope. *(Handing it to TISH)* She didn't open it, either. She left it on the tray.

TISH: This is nuts.

BEX: For sure. *(Beat)* Should we call the Number?

TISH: Now?

BEX: I mean, we *can*. If we need to?

TISH: And say what? "No, we're not ready for someone else. Our first placement is still here. Yeah. Surprise! She's actually having the baby. We *think* she's giving it up for adoption, but we can't be sure since she's barricaded herself in the bedroom and hasn't come out in a month, so she may have changed her mind."

BEX: They probably don't have a protocol for that.

TISH: *(Drily)* Probably not. I think it's on us now.

BEX: I can't believe they haven't called *us*.

TISH: They did. I told you, didn't I? They wanted to see if we were ready for a new placement. I told them we were too busy but to try us again in a few months. I didn't tell them about Anne.

BEX: But why should we have to make excuses? It's not our fault. Also, why is there no follow up? Shouldn't Mama Bear…shouldn't *someone* have called on the date she *should* have left? Did no one tell them when she missed her appointment?

TISH: I don't know. Maybe Anne had told them she didn't need help making her way home... Maybe the clinic gets a lot of no-shows and no one thought to call.

BEX: But, like, shouldn't someone from The Network meet them at the clinic? Just for, you know, solidarity, if nothing else? Does no one even follow up with the clinic to make sure these women show up? I have to say, I'm disappointed in The Network. It doesn't seem like they're very thorough. It's not...what I thought I'd signed up for.

TISH: Yeah, I think we've established that The Network is not, in fact, prepared for every... / exigency.

BEX: *(Simultaneously)* Situation. Yeah.

TISH: Still.

BEX: What?

TISH: Still. I mean, this is more than they can have expected us to take on, right? I mean, we could call them and see what they say...

BEX: No. The Network depends on each link. We'd look like weak links.

TISH: Who cares?

BEX: What if, because of this, they decide not to rely on us anymore? What if we never get the chance to help another woman / because of this?

TISH: Maybe that wouldn't be a bad thing?

BEX: Or maybe it would be unbearable. This is the only good thing I'm doing with my life. Did you see the headlines today?

TISH: Oh, I can't even look anymore. If I had a kid I'd sooner let them watch porn than the news. *(Beat)* Okay.

We won't call. *(Beat)* Looking on the bright side, at least she put my clothes out in the hall.

BEX: How considerate.

TISH: Yeah.

BEX: She hasn't given us anything for laundry, though. You think she's just re-wearing the same things every day?

TISH: She can hand wash stuff in the bathroom, I guess. I mean, who knows what she does when we're out?

BEX: Yeah.

TISH: *(Jealously)* Probably takes long showers.

BEX: We are being awfully good, not complaining about losing the shower, aren't we?

TISH: *(Wryly)* Yes. We're doing great on the good deed front.

BEX: Yeah. *(Beat)* So I know that, like, the last thing we need is to be, like, even more responsible for… but should we be worried, that she hasn't been to the doctor in, like, a month? I was reading, hang on… *(She retrieves "What to Expect When You're Expecting" from somewhere in the piles of clothing, books, paper, etc.)* And it says that she'll need a glucose screening sometime between twenty-four and twenty-eight weeks. So she'll need to go sometime soon, right? Right? *(Beat)* Do you think I should tell her?

TISH: I don't know.

BEX: At least she's eating.

TISH: Yeah…

BEX: Only a few more months.

TISH: Yeah. You know I've added three shifts to cover my share?

BEX: You know I have, too. *(She sighs.)* But, we kind of owe her, right? I mean, we've apparently traumatized her.

TISH: Really, though. I mean it's not like... Isn't enough going to be enough at some point?

BEX: If it were you or me, yeah. But, I mean. I'm not sure she's even left her room. Not even for church! We broke her.

TISH: *(Venting)* So we were mean. Come on. We owe her an apology. Not maid service.

BEX: Well, we agreed that...

TISH: We agreed because she guilt-tripped us into it! She was too weak to lift laundry and too tired to wash dishes...

BEX: So...what do you want to do? Throw her to the wolves? Survival of the fittest?

TISH: I'm just saying, why should we be providing for her? If it were reversed, if you were pregnant, would she be providing for you? Would she take me in? Would she even try to protect me if I needed an abortion?

BEX: So, we only help those who help us?

TISH: We only have so much to go around. And maybe not everyone is equally deserving of our...largesse. Whatever. I'm just saying... Shut up. You're making me feel bad.

BEX: I'm just playing devil's advocate. *(Confessional:)* I'm not really feeling it, either. Helping her. It really would help if she'd seem just a little more...grateful. A little more...in need. A little more...

TISH: A little less entitled.

BEX: A little more deserving.

(BEX *and* TISH *are silent.*)

TISH: *(Changing topic)* I finished my song....

BEX: That's great! I haven't written anything. It's hard to want to write when I'm working all the time. Is it the same song you were working on? From before?

TISH: *(Shaking her head "no")* It's new.

BEX: Is it depressing?

TISH: It's...gritty and realistic.

BEX: *(Encouraging)* That sounds very commercial.

TISH: Let's hope so. I need a new income stream.

BEX: Can I hear it?

TISH: Um. Okay. *(She gets out her guitar, tunes it, and sings. The song has three chords, max, though she strums a lot.)*
Out my window, city streets are
Flecked with blackened gum,
No gold to find.
Rats in a maze in this manmade canyon,
We shuffle through as if we're blind.

And I don't care about my neighbor.
I barely care about myself...

And time...is ticking by.
I'm watching life just pass me by.
Will I make a dent before I die?
Or just stand by?

BEX: That's...deep. Really. True.

TISH: Thanks.

BEX: Is it about...is it inspired by...?

TISH: Just stuff I was thinking. Feeling. It's not, like, literal.

BEX: *(Checking the time)* Shit. My shift.

TISH: Me too. I told Emily I'd cover for her. Get some more hours.

(The rest of the conversation occurs as BEX *and* TISH *change into their black pants and shirts.)*

BEX: Oh good. More hours. We're gonna need a longer day for all these extra hours.

TISH: Right?

BEX: It's too bad we don't have employee of the month. It'd have to be us.

TISH: *(Sardonic.)* Then we'd have something to brag about at the five year. *(Beat. Mustering generosity)* We should try to get her some vegetables or something. I worry she's, like, only eating muffins.

BEX: *(Agreeing, warmly)* It can't be good for her diabetes screen. She had the tomato soup I made, though. *(Correcting herself)* Campbell's made.

TISH: Aw.

BEX: I don't want her to, like, get sick or something.

TISH: No, it's sweet. You're, like, all nurture-y.

BEX: That's me. Earth mother Bex. *(Looking at the time and panicking)* Crap. We'd better split a cab.

*(*BEX *and* TISH *move quickly to the door to exit and as she opens the door,* BEX *pauses to pick up another package.)*

BEX: There's another one.

TISH: Where are they coming from?

BEX: *(Looking at the package)* Amazon.

TISH: I mean, how is she ordering stuff? No one else knows she's here. And, like...?

BEX: Maybe she stole a credit card as she was leaving town.

TISH: This is fucking crazy. (*Nonetheless, she rushes offstage to drop the package at* ANNE's *door.*)

(TISH *returns and she and* BEX *exit in a hurry, locking the door behind them. After several moments,* ANNE *enters. She looks different, no longer the tentative fish-out-of-water from the first scenes. She's dressed a little less modestly too, in New-York-appropriate attire, and she's carrying several empty boxes. She calmly carries them over to the door and sets them down on an empty box that was already there, to be taken to recycling.*)

(*She looks around and realizes she's left her purse in her room. She exits to her room and returns, pulling a phone out of her purse and sending a text as she strolls toward the door. She looks around one last time to make sure she hasn't forgotten anything, fixes her hair in the mirror and leaves, locking the door behind her.*)

Scene 6

(*37 weeks.* TISH's *things have disappeared, but* BEX's *things are now in their place.* ANNE's *belongings have taken over even more of the room. There are now dozens of opened and unopened packages, and a new pile of empty boxes beside the door.* BEX *stands at the coffee table. In front of her is a tray with the lunch she has made for* ANNE, *and she stands studying a bottle of pre-natal vitamins.* TISH *enters.*)

TISH: (*Entering*) Yikes. Want me to take these to recycling?

BEX: Would you? I'm trying to figure out these vitamins. Thanks.

(TISH *drops her bag, picks up the boxes and staggers out to the recycling. After a few moments she returns and watches* BEX, *who continues to puzzle out the ingredient list.*)

TISH: You're gonna be a good mommy someday.

BEX: Haha.

TISH: Look how you're taking care of Anne.

BEX: Well, we're getting into the home stretch now, right? I can't even. Are these the right vitamins?

TISH: *(Coming over, looking, nodding)* "Pre-natals."

BEX: They look different from the last bottle.

TISH: Different brand?

BEX: I don't remember the last ones having all this iron.

TISH: *(Shrugging)* Pregnant women need iron, I guess.

BEX: I just wonder if these are specially formulated for anemic women. Is Anne anemic?

TISH: "Is Anne anemic?" How would I know?

BEX: I guess it can't hurt to have extra iron. *(She sets the bottle down.)* Des left me a message.

TISH: Oh?

BEX: She said she's not planning to renew our lease after it ends next month. *(Beat)* You gave her the check for this month, right?

TISH: Yeah. No. Of course I did.

BEX: Yeah. I just wondered. I mean, maybe she's selling the building or something, but her tone sounded…not very friendly.

TISH: So we'll call her back. Maybe she just wants to raise the rent. I mean, I can't imagine she'll get that much more for this shithole—the dryer in the basement barely works and, like the hallway? Those crooked stairs? That has to be a code violation.

BEX: For sure.

TISH: Do you think anyone's complaining about us? Like a noise complaint or…?

BEX: We're never here!

TISH: Well, but Anne's here. Still.

BEX: But, I mean, she's like a ghost. Anyhow, she'll be gone in a couple of months.

TISH: We'll just call Des. I'm sure she just wants to, like, negotiate. I mean, we're good tenants! We're good people.

BEX: I guess…I spoke with Mama Bear, too.

TISH: You called her? Without talking to me?

BEX: *(Shaking her head)* She called. They need to find placements so she wanted to try us again.

TISH: Did you tell her about…

BEX: Of course I didn't. I mean, we want her to keep sending us people. *(Beat. Sincerely)* We do, right?

(Beat. TISH doesn't answer.)

BEX: Anyhow. I made up a story that work suddenly got nuts for us and we couldn't be here enough to host a new person yet. *(Beat)* It wasn't a complete lie. *(Sadly)* I didn't want her to think we failed.

TISH: *(Lovingly)* Oh, Bex. We didn't fail. *We* didn't make Anne change her mind. *(Rallying)* If anything, whatever screening, whatever procedure they used, didn't vet *her* enough. I think maybe for that reason alone, you should have just told Mama Bear. I mean, they need to fix their process! What if this is happening everywhere? *(Spiraling)* What if it is a plot by right wing extremists to, like, fill up our homes with people who plan to have their babies, just so there's nowhere for desperate women to go?

BEX: I don't think that is happening.

TISH: Why not? It's not like the conspirators would tell the news. And our people can't admit to being duped. Or cop to The Network's existence. So we wouldn't even know if that was happening.

BEX: Tish! I don't have time for you losing your mind. Deedee is getting her hip replaced. So I get another shift! Yay! But the downside is I have slept three hours in the last twenty-four and I have to be back at work in two hours.

TISH: Okay. So take a nap.

BEX: You're standing in my bedroom! Can you just give me some space?

TISH: Fine. But I don't think we should let them turn us against each other. Then they win.

BEX: They've won already! I give up. I give up. *(She lies down on the couch without taking off her shoes or anything and puts a pillow over her head.)*

TISH: *(Chastened)* Okay. Okay. Um. Should I...okay. I'll just...

(TISH takes the tray and adds a prenatal vitamin and picks it up and starts off toward ANNE's room. Before she goes, she carefully balances the tray and dims the lights. A few minutes later she runs back in and turns the lights all the way back on.)

TISH: Bex! Get up!

(Before BEX can voice her outrage, TISH speaks:)

TISH: She's gone. She's gone! What does that mean? Where can she be?

BEX: What? When...

TISH: Her DOOR was open! And she's gone.

BEX: Ok. Um. How long has she been gone? Maybe she went for a walk. I mean, just because we're never here to see her go out doesn't mean she never does. Maybe church? Did she eat her breakfast?

TISH: I don't remember.

BEX: This morning. When you cleared the tray. Was there still food on it?

TISH: Um…yes, but that's not, like, unusual. Right? I mean, when has she ever cleared her plate?

BEX: Did she eat any at all?

TISH: Maybe?

BEX: Okay. Well she ate dinner last night. Some of it. So she's been gone less than twenty-four hours.

TISH: Why does that…? You think we're going to file a missing persons report?

BEX: I mean, I guess? If we need to.

TISH: She's nearly at her due date!

BEX: So okay. We'll leave her a note and tell her it's an emergency and she needs to call us and if she doesn't, by then, by whatever time we decide, then we call the police.

TISH: We can't. We *can't*.

BEX: But if she's…

TISH: Her parents don't even know she's here. She's a minor. Probably. Anyhow. What do we do?

BEX: Maybe she's okay? Maybe she…

TISH: Do you really think she took a walk? She hasn't left in months! We bring her food on a tray, for heaven's sake. Something must be wrong.

BEX: So. What do we do?

TISH: We go looking for her. Right? Don't you think?

BEX: Are you on tonight?

TISH: Yes, but not until nine.

BEX: Okay. Okay. So…we'll split up now and look for her and if we don't find her by my shift you keep looking and if you don't find her, I'll look again when I'm off and if we *still* don't find her, we use the Number.

TISH: I don't even know where to look.

BEX: Well, we have to try. Otherwise, our only option is the Number.

TISH: And they don't even know she's still here.

BEX: Don't you think?

TISH: I guess. Yes. Do you need to change?

BEX: No. Don't judge. Let's go.

(BEX *and* TISH *start offstage just as the door opens. There is* ANNE. *She is now very visibly pregnant. They all freeze for a long moment, considering each other.*)

BEX: *(Furious)* Do you have any idea how worried we've been?

TISH: You have given Bex a heart attack!

BEX: Tish and I have been so worried!

ANNE: *(Dryly)* Are you gonna ground me?

BEX: *(Turning to* TISH*)* Can we do that?

ANNE: I saw the doctor. I thought you'd be pleased.

BEX: *(Relieved)* You saw the doctor? What did he say?

ANNE: She. *(Deliberately pushing* BEX/TISH*'s buttons:)* Women can be doctors now, too.

BEX: What did she say?

ANNE: *(Defiant)* Nothing. *(Relenting)* The baby's head is in the right place so that's good. She's worried about swelling though. She wants me on bedrest.

TISH: *(Sarcastic)* Oh no. Does that mean we'll have to wait on you hand and...oh wait.

ANNE: *(Deliberate, testing)* If you want me to find somewhere else, I can see if there's a shelter somewhere. I'm sure since I'm pregnant I'd be high on the list for a bed...

BEX: *(Knowing she's being manipulated, but softening anyway)* No. Of course not. You stay here. We were just worried. Would you like a sandwich?

ANNE: I'm fine. I'm gonna / go lie down, I think.

TISH: *(Anticipating, she speaks simultaneously.)* Go lie down. Yes. Do that.

ANNE: *(To* TISH, *explaining)* She said I need to keep myself from getting too stressed. For the baby.

BEX: Okay. Um. *(Slight beat)* Did she check your protein and sugar levels?

ANNE: *(Continuing, to* TISH*)* So I'd appreciate it if you'd keep your...resentment to yourself.

TISH: *(Incredulous)* My resentment? *(Sarcastic)* Why should I be resentful? I try to do a kind thing for a stranger—I'm sorry, Bex. *(Correcting herself)* We try to do a kind thing for a stranger, for a woman in need. We're trying to be Good Samaritans here, and along comes someone who not only walks on our cloak but then steals it from us.

ANNE: *(Outraged)* I have never stolen—

TISH: Not, like, literally. But I think it's convenient, it's super amazingly lucky for you, isn't it? That while you can't get a job and have no money for rent or utilities or anything—and no, we didn't ask you for any when we thought you were staying for a weekend, a week tops— But you somehow can stay here for almost five, eventually eight months, and contribute nothing, but you can magically find money for a giant *plushie*— *(She indicates one.)*

ANNE: It's a unicorn riding an apple! Like, the BIG APPLE? And it's a present! For the baby!

TISH: *(Gesturing again)* And I guess the baby needs sunglasses? And a freaking purse?

ANNE: I need things too.

BEX: Seriously?

ANNE: *(Gesturing around her)* These things? *(Shaking her head)* No one back home could have imagined these things…but they sell them here!

TISH: You're making my point for me! You're shopping up a storm buying completely unnecessary things! Shiny things, pretty things, but come on, these are not things you actually need for, say, your baby or your body or anything. You're willing and able to pay for these things—

ANNE: *(Daring)* Well…I'm not.

TISH: What?

ANNE: *I'm* not.

TISH: You're not what?

ANNE: Paying.

BEX: I don't understand. Do you just, like, walk out of the store with…? Are you *(She whispers the word) shoplifting?*

ANNE: *(Appalled)* No! Of course not. That's stealing.

BEX: Okay.

TISH: Okay..?

(Long beat. BEX and TISH wait for ANNE to clarify.)

BEX: Did your, uh, baby Daddy—?

ANNE: My… No!

BEX: Oh my God. Are you…? Do you have, like, a sugar daddy? Are you *(She whispers.) a prostitute?*

ANNE: What? Of course not. Look at me!

TISH: Then how are you paying for—

BEX: You have a rich aunt! And she gave you her credit card for emergencies!

ANNE: Warmer!

TISH: How much did she give you?

ANNE: I don't have a rich aunt.

TISH: The church. The church took up a collection for—

ANNE: Nope.

BEX: *(Confounded)* Oh! Did The Network…?

ANNE: No.

TISH: Okay… Who is paying for all this stuff?

ANNE: I am.

(A beat)

TISH: How.

ANNE: Cash. Credit card.

TISH: You applied for a credit card? You don't even—

ANNE: *(Delighted)* No. They *gave* it to me.

TISH: I'm sorry. People just gave you a credit card?

ANNE: I really shouldn't say anymore. They said to keep it a secret.

TISH: Who did?

(ANNE says nothing.)

BEX: I don't understand. Who pays for the card?

(ANNE says nothing.)

TISH: No one is supposed to know you are here. Right? I mean, you told your family you were on a mission for your new church.

ANNE: I did.

BEX: *(Attempting to be helpful)* Right, okay. So…

TISH: Does anyone know you're here?

BEX: Also, because, I mean, if people know that we're hosting you, and if, like, your family or whatever knows you're NOT here on a church project and, like, they go looking for someone to blame, then we wouldn't want them to trace anything to The Network, right?

(ANNE *shrugs.*)

BEX: I mean, right?

TISH: *(To* ANNE:*)* Are you being cavalier about this? Because they were very clear about that at our training, weren't they, Bex?

BEX: They were, Tish.

TISH: Speaking of our training, do you remember, Bex, the kind of women we could expect we'd be hosting?

BEX: *(As if reciting from memory)* "The typical woman is in an early stage. She is often already a mother. She is unable to provide for an additional child and she is in need of a quick and immediate intervention so she can return home to her children." That doesn't sound right. Quick *and* immediate? I think I'm remembering that wrong.

TISH: No. That's fine. That's the gist. Quick and immediate. Would you say, Bex, that this has been a quick and immediate kind of help we've provided?

BEX: Um…

TISH: Nor do I. *(Turing to* ANNE, *falsely solicitous)* I hope we're not making you uncomfortable. But I think this needs to be a bit more of a two-way street. And, I suppose, I'm just thinking that it would enable us to take better care of you if we understood where you were coming from.

ANNE: I'm not supposed to say where—

TISH: Not literally.

BEX: Not literally.

ANNE: *(Wincing)* I think this is what the doctor meant by a stressful conversation. I think—

TISH: Oh. I see. Well. I—

ANNE: You got mad when I asked before, but I think I really do need to lie—

TISH: Haven't you been already? Lying?

ANNE: About what?

TISH: Where are you getting the money? Are you a spy? Are you here to infiltrate The Network?

BEX: Tish.

ANNE: *(Slightly distracted)* What? No. What? Are you crazy?

TISH: No, I am not.

BEX: She's just tired and emotional.

TISH: Do not speak for me.

BEX: I was just—

TISH: I don't need an interpreter. Where did you get the money, Anne?

ANNE: I don't. I don't have to tell you.

TISH: Aha!

BEX: Hang on. That doesn't mean… *(To ANNE)* Look, are you getting paid to screw up The Network?

ANNE: What? No. Of course not.

TISH: There is no "of course" about it.

BEX: Please. *(To ANNE)* Can you understand why this is confusing? Why we're feeling a little suspicious?

ANNE: *(Sharply. Masking her physical discomfort)* Your suspicion is not my problem.

BEX: *(Outraged by this response)* I'm sorry, what? Our suspicion is not your problem?

(A drop of water falls on her from the ceiling. BEX looks up.)

BEX: Shit.

(BEX looks up and then takes off to grab a pot from the kitchen as ANNE responds.)

ANNE: It is not my problem. It wasn't long ago you didn't believe I was even pregnant. I'm pregnant. I'm having a baby. This is a dying world, but you go on living your decadent lives—

TISH: We aren't the ones buying crap we don't need!

(BEX reenters and places the pot on the ground under the leak. It drips again.)

TISH: We aren't the ones sitting back reading magazines while other people work three shifts to keep us fed and in prenatal vitamins!

BEX: Oh, and my ankles are swollen too, by the way!

TISH: We're working to the bone to—

ANNE: To the bone? You don't even know—ah! *(She freezes.)*

BEX: And you do?

TISH: Because of you some other woman has not had a place to go. Because of you—

(TISH pauses, suddenly aware that the drip from the ceiling has become a steady trickle.)

TISH: Because of you...

ANNE: I think. I need. I think I need—

BEX: Just tell us where you got the money. *(Beat)* Who is paying for all of this?

ANNE: I think—

BEX: *(Sarcastic)* You think?

ANNE: I think the baby's coming. *(She gestures at her pants, which have been darkening as her water has broken.)*

TISH: *(Still looking at the ceiling)* Oh my God.

BEX: *(Looking at* ANNE*)* Oh my God.

ANNE: *(Shutting her eyes as a stronger contraction comes)* Oh my God.

*(*ANNE *braces herself against the table as the contraction comes. As she does, chunks of plaster fall from the ceiling and water floods down into the apartment from above.)*

TISH: *(Startled by* ANNE's *"blasphemy," looking at her)* Anne?

*(*ANNE *starts to pray.* TISH *looks at* BEX. BEX *looks at the ceiling and then back at* TISH.*)*

Scene 7

*(*DES *stands looking at the ceiling and occasionally taking notes as* BEX *wordlessly gathers wet stuffed animals and clothing and magazines from around the room and spreads them to dry or examines them and puts them in one of several trash bags.* TISH *watches* DES *with great concentration. This continues in silence for a very, very long time. Finally,* DES *finishes examining the ceiling and turns toward the hallway, looking back over her shoulder at* BEX *and then directing her attention to* TISH, *asking to check the other rooms.)*

DES: May I...?

TISH: I don't see how...?

(Before TISH *can finish her thought and say "that's relevant?"* DES, *unsmiling, raises an eyebrow.* TISH *wordlessly acquiesces, and* DES *goes around the corner, out of sight, to inspect the rest of the apartment.)*

BEX: Do—?

TISH: Ssh!

(TISH *wanders over to watch from afar as* DES *continues assessing.* BEX *continues cleaning. She tries from time to time to catch* TISH's *eye, but* TISH *remains vigilant, watching what she can of* DES's *investigation.*)

DES: *(Returning)* Obviously there's some…water, coming from upstairs. I'm going to have to call the plumber and we're going to have to see where it's coming from, if it's coming from outside, or if Mrs Romero—

BEX: Thank you.

DES: *(Annoyed at the interruption)* Or if it's from Mrs Romero's fixtures. Whatever. It has to be fixed. I will have to fix it.

TISH: Thank you.

DES: Be that as it may. You are clearly in violation of the lease. *(Gesturing at all the stuff everywhere)* I can't imagine you're going to argue that only the two of you have been living here?

(*As* BEX *and* TISH *open their mouths to protest:*)

DES: For months. And you know what? I don't really give a damn. I like to think I'm pretty cool about most shit, but that was in the lease and I'm pretty sure that this… Noachian fucking flood didn't just start yesterday—

BEX: We did text you…

DES: About something "funky" with the plaster! Come on. You can't really be that dumb. You just didn't report it because you were more worried about your own rent violations than you were about the condition of my building.

BEX: *(Insulted)* Hey! *(Controlling herself)* Can I…? *(When* DES *doesn't stop her, she begins)* Look, first of all, not that

it makes any difference in terms of our legal.... but we
did actually let you know when we saw something
was up with the ceiling.

(Before DES *can reply:)*

BEX: And yes, someone has been staying with us, but
we haven't been renting to her. We weren't earning
income. We were just helping out a friend. Well, not
really a friend. In fact, we don't even know her—

DES: Don't care. *(Gently)* Look, the real estate taxes
have totally gone up in this neighborhood, so it was
time anyhow... Come on. You've had a really good
deal. A really fucking excellent deal. *(Attempting a joke)*
And you know, I remember when I was young and
stupid. That's why I rented to such obviously young
and stupid—

BEX: That's not...nevermind.

DES: But I'm not a kid anymore. I have, like, adult—

TISH: But, like...we're friends, aren't we?

DES: Sure we are. *(Turning to look at her)* What does
Avery do for a living?

TISH: He's...a, um, he does, like, consulting? Or
something?

DES: Or something. Yeah. He's an immigration
attorney. His clients have been known to pay us
in baked goods. So we kind of need not to have
catastrophic leaks, you see? And we kind of need to
get market rate on the apartments we have. Whatever.
Look. I don't want to be a tool about this. You can have
a week to get your stuff together...

BEX: A week?

DES: I mean, pretty obviously I'm going to have to do
some major repairs so it's not going to be habitable
for a while. I'm doing you a favor actually. I mean,

it's not very habitable now. I think you're better off finding something else anyway. As I told you over the phone, it was time. I wasn't going to continue the lease anyhow.

TISH: But where are we going to go?

BEX: Wait, wait. Des. Look. I'm not even worried about *us*.

(As TISH *starts to protest,* BEX *barrels ahead.)*

BEX: I mean, I *am*. Where we are going to go I don't even know, but here's the thing. Our…illegal renter—

TISH: *(Urgently)* Bex. We can't.

DES: *(Pausing, interested)* What about her?

TISH: *Bex. Des.* I'm sorry, but we really can't discuss her with you. *(Reconsidering. Carefully)* But she's… having a medical issue.

DES: Uh-huh.

TISH: And so. Actually, when you were arriving, we were just going through her things to see what we could bring her. She's in the hospital. So she won't—

DES: I see. *(She picks up some of the clothing and accessories from the "not destroyed" pile.)*

BEX: Actually, those are hers. Can you put them back?

DES: I could bring them to her. At the hospital. While you're cleaning up here.

TISH: Oh. Um. That's…I appreciate your offer to help, but we'll do that.

DES: No. You stay and clean. I'll bring these to her. *(Deliberately)* To Anne.

BEX: Wait…?

TISH: I'm confused.

BEX: You've met her?

(DES *doesn't answer.*)

BEX: Wait. You've met her? (*Urgently*) Then you know she's gonna need a week or so to recover. When she's back. From the hospital.

TISH: Or longer. Actually.

(DES *doesn't answer.* TISH *looks at* BEX *and decides to go for it.*)

TISH: Des? If you've met her, you know she's…in a… she's pregnant. So here's the thing. She's planning to give the baby up for adoption. So that's gonna take time. And she's gonna need a place to stay until all that's finalized. So maybe you can wait to repair the place. Maybe just fix the ceiling but wait on the floors, say, until she's finalized things and she's ready to go home. And then we'll all leave.

DES: She is staying, uh, with me until this place is cleaned up, I guess. But then, here. You have to go.

BEX: Wait, but…

TISH: Are you kidding?

DES: (*Shrugging*) I'm sorry. She'd rather live here without you.

TISH: That's crazy. It's our apartment.

DES: Well, technically…

BEX: It's your apartment. Yes. But we've been good tenants until now. I mean, except for lying about Anne. And maybe we need more rugs. Right? And *she* can't pay market rate, I assure you! So, like…I mean, you don't even know her! She's not any better than us!

TISH: She's actually a terrible roommate. A terrible tenant.

DES: I see.

TISH: I thought we got along, Des. I thought, you know, we were ok. I'm telling you, she's a sponging little parasite and she –

DES: But she's his birth mother.

BEX: Yes, she's a mother. But she's giving it up—

DES: And for that, we are so very grateful. Avery and me.

BEX: What...? I don't understand...

DES: She's the biological mother of our child, and Avery and I—

TISH: What?

BEX: You're not from the Upper East Side!

DES: That's...correct...?

TISH: She's using you.

DES: *(Shrugging)* Maybe. Probably. You should see her credit card bills. But, you know, the adoption process is expensive. And lengthy. And complicated. And we have been trying to have a baby every which way for three years now, and then this fell into our laps and we are grateful. I'm grateful. To you. For helping take care of her. Thank you. But I'm afraid you can't stay here now and she doesn't want you here when she gets back. *(She gathers up some of the toys/accessories)* You can take whatever time you need to gather your stuff. But the contractor's coming tomorrow, so... Just leave the rest of her things. I'll help her sort them later. Oh. And the water won't be on again until Thursday, until they've finished investigating the pipes and the branch lines...so just a heads up. I mean, you can still stay the week, but... *(She shrugs and gathers her things)* And I'm obviously going to need to keep your deposit. I'm sure you understand that. You can just leave the keys with Silva. I'm sorry it's ending this way, but really, I wish only good things for you. Really. Maybe I'll see you around the neighborhood. Peace.

(DES *exits. There's a long beat as a stunned* BEX *and* TISH *try to process what just happened.*)

BEX: Wow. I thought Des liked us.

TISH: Des is a crappy human being. "Peace!"

BEX: What are we going to do? We're never gonna… Shit. I'm gonna be Deedee aren't I? Oh God.

TISH: I need to think. I can't think.

BEX: We are so screwed.

TISH: And the water soaked my stash.

BEX: (*Checking her phone for the time*) I have to go to work anyway.

TISH: Oh God, me too. What time is it?

(*TISH checks her phone and stares at it for a moment before showing it to* BEX.)

TISH: The Network called.

BEX: You're kidding.

(TISH *shows* BEX *the screen.*)

TISH: Nope.

BEX: I can't believe it.

TISH: This is some exquisite timing.

BEX: Seriously.

TISH: (*Swiping at her phone*) Delete.

BEX: Eff that.

TISH: Seriously!

BEX: Seriously.

TISH: Save yourselves, bitches.

(TISH *drops her phone in her bag, slicks on some lipstick and throws on a black sweater and a jacket as* BEX *grabs her coat and they hustle out the door. It clicks shut and they lock it.)*

END OF PLAY